PAMPHLETS ON AMERICAN WRITERS · NUMBER 43

UNIVERSITY OF MINNESOTA

⤳ *Sherwood Anderson*

BY BROM WEBER

UNIVERSITY OF MINNESOTA PRESS · MINNEAPOLIS

Printed in the United States of America at
the North Central Publishing Company, St. Paul

Library of Congress Catalog Card Number: 64-64450

Distributed to high schools in the United States by Webster Division
McGraw-Hill Book Company, Inc.
St. Louis   New York   San Francisco   Dallas

PUBLISHED IN GREAT BRITAIN, INDIA, AND PAKISTAN BY THE OXFORD UNIVERSITY
PRESS, LONDON, BOMBAY, AND KARACHI, AND IN CANADA BY THE COPP
CLARK PUBLISHING CO. LIMITED, TORONTO

SHERWOOD ANDERSON

BROM WEBER, professor of English at the University of California, Davis, has edited *An Anthology of American Humor* and *The Letters of Hart Crane*.

Sherwood Anderson

Life, not death, is the great adventure." So reads the inscription engraved on Sherwood Anderson's tombstone in southwestern Virginia in accordance with a request he made not long before his death at sixty-four in 1941. At first glance, the buoyancy of the epitaph seems strangely at variance with the facts of his career. For a few triumphant years after the publication of *Winesburg, Ohio* (1919), Anderson was acclaimed a major figure of modern literature. He was regarded with Theodore Dreiser as a liberator of American letters from the debilitating effects of the genteel tradition. Then, in the mid-1920's, repudiated by critics, abandoned by his early discoverers, parodied by his protégés, he slipped from the foreground, even though his writing continued to influence diverse writers such as Ernest Hemingway, Hart Crane, Erskine Caldwell, Katherine Anne Porter, Henry Miller, William Faulkner, Nathanael West, and James T. Farrell.

Anderson thought humbly of himself at the end as merely a minor artist who had contributed only a minor classic — *Winesburg, Ohio* — to American culture. Still, it was his dedication as an artist that enabled him to sustain his faith in the adventure of life — and fully examined, his career truly justifies his epitaph. It was with grace and justice that Faulkner, responding to an inquiry from a *Paris Review* interviewer in 1956, declared of Anderson's stature: "He was the father of my generation of American writers and the tradition of American writing which our successors will carry on. He has never received his proper evaluation."

The major theme of Anderson's writing is the tragedy of death in life: modern man, lacking personal identity and with his senses anesthetized, has become a spiritless husk unfitted for love of man and community. This perennial theme is common enough in our time, though it was relatively dormant in the late 1910's when Anderson first enunciated it. It became his leitmotiv when, in 1912, at the age of thirty-six, he suffered a nervous breakdown and rejected his past. Thereafter he viewed this event as a symbolic rebirth which had purified him of false values and freed him from the confines of deadening institutions.

The pattern is classic in Western culture. It has recurred often in American life since Puritan times, with special frequency in the nineteenth century after the rise of transcendentalism. But in the 1920's it was somewhat anachronistic for a man to present himself dramatically, not only as artist but also as human being, in the messianic role of someone who had achieved a second birth and now had come forth to utter prophetic truths. Nor did Anderson's lower-class origins in Ohio, his vaunted and obvious lack of education, his emphasis upon the American and the common, his bohemian dress and manners, his concern with lust and love, and his charismatic religious overtones make him more palatable either to the intellectual or to the average man.

The reasons for suspicion are understandable. It followed upon a perversion of the idealism and romanticism of Emerson, Thoreau, and Whitman by nineteenth-century disciples who, regardless of their original motives, too often degenerated into cultists and opportunists. Emerson and Whitman are not responsible for followers who took advantage of the masters' paradoxical universality and founded quasi-religious movements such as New Thought, which misused idealistic concepts to justify materialism. Nor should the masters be blamed for the phenomenon of an Elbert Hubbard, who had publicized his idealistic escape from business in the 1890's in order to pursue a life of pure art, plain living, and high thinking, then proceeded to befoul American culture with a shamelessly commercial literature, handicraft, art, and thought until he sank with the *Lusitania* in 1915. Yet many had been fooled by the Emersonian-Whitmanian pose of Hubbard, with the result that Anderson — who, like Hubbard, came from the Midwest, sported an arty costume, and had also worked in business and advertising — was regarded with some wariness even while his writing was being praised.

In private life, letters, and autobiographical publications, Anderson tenaciously mixed art and life until he became a fictional character for himself and his times. Many supposedly objective details in *A Story Teller's Story* (1924), *Tar* (1926), and the posthumous *Memoirs* (1942) were products of "fancy," a term he used interchangeably with "imagination." He preferred these imaginative constructions to "facts" which he believed concealed "the essence of things." The angry corrections of relatives and friends did not alter his belief that a man's vision of himself and his world contained more meaningful truth than did a birth certificate or an identification card. There was no real ground for embarrassment. In the opening pages of his autobiographical works, readers were forewarned at once about Anderson's method. There is something playful and ingenuous in such typical fictions as his Italian grandmother and his southern father; they happen to be profoundly true in revealing the surprise and shock of a passionate "Ohio Pagan" who couldn't otherwise explain the incongruity of having been spawned in an American Midwest dominated by what he regarded as the chilly values of its "Puritan" New England settlers.

Sherwood Anderson was born on September 13, 1876, in Camden, Ohio. He was the third child of Irwin M. Anderson, who made and sold leather harness, and Emma Smith Anderson. The Anderson family had moved about from town to town in Ohio before Sherwood's birth. A few years after that event, Irwin Anderson's small business failed and the Anderson family resumed its travels. Not until 1884 was a permanent home established, this time in Clyde, a small farm town.

The strain of economic difficulties and wandering seems to have affected the father, who began to drink heavily and was so often unemployed that the family's needs frequently were satisfied only by the children's earnings and the strenuous efforts of their mother. Irwin Anderson as father and fictional character was to be an obsessive and ambivalently treated concern of Sherwood's thought and art. He and the other children would feel that Emma Anderson's death in 1895 might have been caused by her husband's neglect and frivolity. But Irwin was nevertheless lovable, in many respects admirable. His misfortunes had not soured his temper, and he joyfully gave rein to his aptitudes for music, theater, and literature. If a parade or vaudeville performance had to be arranged, Irwin Anderson was the man for the job; he acted; he blew the cornet in a local band; he entranced his friends and children with skillfully told tales. Such a role could excite admiration and respect; there were penalties too — family hardships and the probability that town and family alike would consider one a quixotic clown and fool. It was not until Sherwood Anderson was in his mid-forties that he highly valued what he had earlier feared, namely, his similarity to his father.

Young Sherwood's willingness to take on odd jobs earned him money and the nickname of "Jobby." He worked as a farmhand in the surrounding country; in Clyde as grocery delivery boy, laborer in a newly established bicycle factory, and newsboy, and in various menial capacities in a livery stable and a racehorse stable, where he mingled happily with drivers, jockeys, grooms, and trainers. Though an average student, his various jobs and interests made it difficult for him to attend school regularly; he finally quit high school before graduation.

Anderson's life in Clyde ended when he left in 1896 for Chicago, where his brother Karl had gone earlier. For the next two years, Anderson was a manual laborer in a cold-storage warehouse. With the outbreak of the Spanish-American War, he volunteered for army service in Cuba. His regiment arrived there in January 1899, almost four months after hostilities had ceased. Though he never underwent the combat experience which other American novelists such as Hemingway, John Dos Passos, Thomas Boyd, and Faulkner were to incorporate into their fiction, Anderson had an opportunity to become aware of the problems faced by the individual in a mass society requiring conformity to a single mode of conduct. That Anderson knew how to adjust himself may be gauged from his attainment of a corporal's rank. It was probably this slight success which encouraged a belief — embodied most fully in an early novel, *Marching Men* (1917) — that man as individual was ineffectual until, absorbed into a faceless mass led by a charismatic leader, he contributed his will and body to an invincible social entity.

At loose ends in 1900 after his army service, Sherwood again followed his brother, this time to Springfield, Ohio, where the latter was employed as an artist by the Crowell Publishing Company, which issued mass-circulation magazines. Aware of his need for more education, Anderson in September enrolled at Wittenberg Academy, a preparatory school, where he earned eleven grades of A and three of B for his proficiency in Latin, German, geometry, English, and physics. He was twenty-four years old at the time, but he did not feel it demeaning to pay for his food and lodging by working as a "chore boy" in the

9

boardinghouse where he, Karl, and various editors, artists, advertising men, and teachers resided.

These men and women were the most culturally advanced Anderson had met as yet. Their interests in art and literature, as well as business, uncovered new, if limited, worlds of action and thought for him. But as it happens it was in the field of business that the Springfield group ultimately did most for him. Through the intercession of the advertising manager of Crowell, Anderson was appointed to the Chicago advertising office of the firm as a copywriter. He was among the first and not the last of modern American writers whose imagination and expression have been affected by such experience.

Anderson initially took to advertising with gusto and a belief in the efficacy of the products he touted and the means used to sell them. Businessmen whom he met in his later role as advertising salesman liked him because of his "charm, interest, and sympathy," his physical attractiveness and lively spirit. His mental alertness and sensitivity to the language of the average mind made him an irresistible copywriter. One of his associates related that Anderson "bragged to the office girls that he could get them good husbands by mail-order letters."

The most revealing expression of his attitudes is to be found in the inspirational articles and sketches he contributed to *Agricultural Advertising,* his firm's house organ, during 1903 and 1904. Written in a clumsy, banal style, these pieces on the whole echo the platitudes of popular American business philosophy, uncritically expounding the virtues of industry, acquisition, aggressive competition, optimism, success, and service, while chiding those who prated reform morality and ignored the ethical values and practices of the businessman. Though Anderson in later years would denounce success and extoll failure, he never became an enthusiast of social reform except sporadically during the

1930's. He regarded social liberals and revolutionists as opportunists who concealed their search for power under showers of misleading "talk." During the 1930's, when most of those who had championed his work were involved in leftist activities, his unwillingness to commit himself fully to radical programs led to sharp criticism or neglect of his last writings.

Whatever confidence and success advertising brought Anderson, and it also enabled him in 1904 to marry Cornelia Lane, the daughter of a wealthy Ohio wholesaler of footwear, the afflatus of sales promotion did not continue to satisfy him. His rising sense of frustration was fanned by the genteel achievements of his wife, who had been graduated from Western Reserve University, possessed the traditional knowledge of literature and the arts which he lacked, and had even studied in Europe. In a conversation of the mid-1900's with a Chicago advertising associate before departing on a business trip, Anderson said that he had decided to choose between becoming "a millionaire or an artist." He explained that, "if only a man will put the making of money above all other things in life," wealth could be attained. The role of an artist was more difficult, "but if it is in a fellow, he can do it. I don't know what I shall do — paint, sculp, maybe write. But I think I will come back determined on an artistic career."

The transition from copy writing to literature as art, which Anderson was to make, seemed easy and natural to him because in both language is manipulated to give an illusion of meaningful reality. His view was implicit in an advertising man's comment on a verbally gifted railroad man in one of Anderson's *Agricultural Advertising* sketches: "He knows how to use words and that's why I think he'd make an advertising man. How to use words, and say, Mr. Cowman, that's what advertising is, just using words; just picking them out like that fellow picked out his swear words and then dropping them down in just the right place so they seem to mean something. I don't want you to be making fun of that brakeman. . . . He's a word man, that brakeman is, and words are the greatest things ever invented."

Anderson's reverent attitude toward language was a wholesome sign of his promise as a writer. In the 1900's, it was useful to him because of his limited vocabulary and his unfamiliarity with the range of rhetorical devices to be found in literature. But his emphasis upon "words" as self-sufficient entities, and his lack of concern with their meaning, foreshadowed his later obsessive preoccupation with them. As he struggled unsuccessfully with the expression of ideas and emotional nuances in his first two novels, he came to believe that his failure resulted from the faulty character of his words rather than from the absence of that profound imaginative experience which willy-nilly finds vivid expression even in a limited language. "There is a story. — I cannot tell it. — I have no words," he would write in 1921.

This was to an extent only an element of the guileless and natural literary personality Anderson fashioned as a self-portrait. It came properly indeed from one whose advertising experience had shown him that words could be used without responsible interest in their human meaning and was determined not to repeat his errors. On the one hand then, Anderson's love and fear of the word stimulated great stylistic purity; on the other hand, this ambivalence also led on occasion to a "basic mistrust of language itself" and to the artistically destructive belief that "reality remains ultimately inexpressible" to which Anderson alluded in the epigraph of *A New Testament* (1927): "They talked and their lips said audible words but the voices of their inner selves went on uninterrupted."

Anderson continued to nourish hopes of an artistic career while adjusting himself to the responsibilities of a bourgeois husband who had fathered three children. Leaving Chicago in 1906, he returned to northern Ohio. During the next six years, he managed a mail-order business in Cleveland and later two paint manufacturing firms. In dress, country club membership, church attendance, and all other externals, Anderson conformed to the standards of respectable convention. But first secretly, in the night-time privacy of an attic at home, and later openly, in his office and elsewhere, Anderson began to write with such industry and devotion that friends and business acquaintances could not help becoming aware of his double existence. He centered more and more energy in his writing as an estrangement from his wife deepened in intensity and as financial difficulties made it likely that his business was going to fail.

On November 27, 1912, Anderson left his office in Elyria, Ohio, suddenly and was not heard from again until he turned up in Cleveland on December 1, disheveled and in a state of shock. In the Cleveland hospital to which he was taken, examining physicians diagnosed his condition as a mental collapse. Although he recovered quickly, the event was a turning point. He severed connections with his manufacturing business and, in order to support himself and his family, returned to his old Chicago advertising job in February 1913, bringing with him the manuscripts of *Windy McPherson's Son, Marching Men,* and other works.

Anderson's version of his departure from Elyria, presented in an article entitled "When I Left Business for Literature" (*Century*, August 1924) and incorporated in *A Story Teller's Story*, became a classic anecdote in the 1920's and 1930's. For Anderson and some younger writers, it symbolized the heroism of rebellion against the materialistic values of a business-dominated culture. Predictably, however, not all of his version was accurate. As he viewed the event in 1924 and later in the *Memoirs*, he ignored his psychic breakdown and slighted his precarious financial state, thus giving the impression that his flight had resulted from a wholly conscious decision to repudiate wealth and embrace art. To this extent, his story was misleading. But he also stated the essential truth and it was unimpeachable: after much struggle, he had committed himself to a disinterested life of art and thereafter had flaunted his disbelief in the moral integrity and social value of the advertising copy he continued to write so brilliantly until 1922.

Anderson's first two novels are apprentice efforts. He was never proud of these books, even when they were published. Later, in the *Memoirs*, he called them imitative and "immature." It is regrettable that Anderson permitted them to be published without extensive improvement, for in 1915, before their appearance, he was already writing the first brilliant tales of *Winesburg, Ohio* and undoubtedly was aware of the weaknesses of the novels. At this time, as later in his career, Anderson made the mistake of publishing work which did not reflect his achieved talent and thus gave rise to mistaken impressions of his progress and promise.

Although Anderson later said that he had tricked the reader with a happy ending, *Windy McPherson's Son* (1916) has a tragic or at least an ambivalent ending. Sam McPherson's search for meaning in life concludes in a chaos of emptiness and negation. The dominant tone is one of darkness and frustration, steadily increasing in intensity. Young Sam — eager to acquire wealth — flees to Chicago from his Iowa village and becomes a robber baron. He is diverted from his unsatisfying material quest after meeting a perfect woman who convinces him that he will achieve fulfillment by creating perfect children with her. This eugenic goal is abandoned after she proves incapable of giving birth. Sam returns to business and finance, attaining vast power but no more satisfaction than before. He rules faceless men and cannot discover his own face. The social reform faddishly taken up by his frustrated wife does not attract him. In all action, idealistic or selfish, theories are discarded and the urge for power nakedly revealed as motive force. Sam flees Chicago in desperation.

Dressed in the costume of a Whitmanian rough, Sam McPherson wanders about as vagabond and workman "to seek Truth, to seek God" among the common people. He finds labor confused and its leaders power-hungry. Love is missing. Dissipation and vice have destroyed the moral character of the people. Sam cannot find God in man or society, thus repeating a boyhood experience when he had read the Bible and discovered that "Christ's simple message" of love and community had been rejected by the Iowa villagers. Wearied by "thinking" and searching, Sam loses faith in hope.

The resurgent theme of fertility rouses Sam briefly. He brings three neglected children home to his lonely wife, who has found solace, ironically, in the writing of Emersonian "articles about life and conduct." Upon Sam's return, she derides them as "pettiness." Both hope that, with the aid of the children, they may be able to realize their earlier unifying aim of nurturing perfect beings for the future. But the concluding paragraph of the novel is far from hopeful. The last lines are unmistakably despairing: "A shudder ran through his body and he had the impulse to run away into the darkness, to begin again, seeking, seeking. Instead he turned and going through the door, walked across the lighted room to sit again with Sue at his own table and to try to force himself back into the ranks of life." Nothing in the novel promises that Sam will be able to remain in the light.

Anderson's later weakness as a novelist is evident in his inability to make Sam McPherson see, feel, and evaluate his experience with concrete details and expanding complexity. Sam yearns to break loose from the sterilizing confines of existence but his spirit is subdued by a numbing sameness that renders him unfit for observation and participation. Had Anderson created suspense by involving Sam in a more detailed inner drama of conflicting emotion and idea or a more detailed outer drama of disturbing social interaction, the tragic conclusion would have embodied a persuasive force. As it is, Sam's impotent isolation ultimately tends to become more pathetic than deeply tragic.

The limited dimension of Sam is paralleled in most of the other characters, who remain undeveloped sentimental stereotypes. Some of these recur with haunting regularity in Anderson's later work: the kind, maternal schoolteacher who talks about books and art; the loved and hated braggart father; the exhausted, sacrificial mother who dies too soon; the wife who doesn't understand her husband or give herself to love; the promiscuous woman who cheapens physical passion.

The strengths of *Windy McPherson's Son* reside primarily in the first eight chapters dealing with Sam's village life before his quest for money and power in Chicago. This section of the book might almost be a discarded draft of *Winesburg, Ohio*. Many sentences are packed with the hum of feeling and have a Biblical cadence; "tears" express a specific emotional reaction and are not just plashed for dubious sentimental effect; imagery and diction generally are free from cliché and stereotype. Three characters anticipate the figures of *Winesburg, Ohio* in their expressiveness, the depth of their passion and insight, and the incongruity between their powers and their limited achievement.

John Telfer is an articulate and vivid man whose failure as painter has led him to a richer role: artist of living. His talk of

Whitman, love, purpose, and ideals almost sways Sam from devotion to money; it is Telfer who emphasizes the difference between corn as a symbol of materialism and corn as a symbol of the *élan vital*: "I see the long corn rows with the men and the horses half hidden, hot and breathless, and I think of a vast river of life. I catch a breath of the flame that was in the mind of the man who said, 'The land is flowing with milk and honey.'" But Telfer cannot affect Sam's future any more than Sam's emotionally profound father, Windy McPherson, or the "savage and primitive" Mike McCarthy. The latter delights in fertilizing village wives whose miserly husbands have forsworn "carnal love," and the children it produces, in favor of saving money. Like Telfer, both have virtues worth emulating. Yet each is ultimately defeated, Windy by his hollow pretensions and Mike by the uncontrollable passion which leads to his murdering a resentful cuckold.

Anderson's second published novel, *Marching Men* (1917), although structurally flawed, is noteworthy for its stylistic fluency and its fusion of ideas and dramatic action. This is not surprising, for Anderson was by no means a literary *naïf* in the mid-1910's as he and others have suggested. In Chicago after 1912 he had come to know such literary figures as Floyd Dell, Carl Sandburg, Margaret Anderson, and Ben Hecht; Anderson also contributed to the *Little Review*, along with *Poetry* the most important American "little magazine" of the 1910's. There are references to Poe, Browning, Carlyle, Keats, Balzac, Whitman, and Mark Twain in *Windy McPherson's Son*, as well as allusions to unspecified French, Russian, and other European writers; in a 1923 letter, Anderson asserted that he had read Turgenev about 1911 and Tolstoi and Dostoevski afterward. Shakespeare and Dante are mentioned in *Marching Men*. According to Anderson's *Memoirs*, he was already familiar with the novels of

Bennett, Wells, Hardy, and Moore. His brother Karl had introduced him to Gertrude Stein's experimental *Tender Buttons* (1914) soon after its appearance; he had read her *Three Lives* (1909) earlier.

Marching Men is a social novel. In it Anderson examined the destructive impact of industrialism in a Pennsylvania coal-mining town upon a sensitive boy and traced the harmful effect of his warped personality upon society. Ironically nicknamed "Beaut" because of his gawkiness and physical ugliness, Norman McGregor's lyrical response to nature and his affectionate spirit are brutally crushed. Beaut McGregor grows to hate man and society. In Chicago he finds opportunity, as lawyer and charismatic leader, to obtain revenge for his youthful sufferings. Viewing urban, industrial man as a dehumanized shell, he accelerates the dehumanization by organizing the masses into battalions which, subjected to strict discipline, march in military fashion. His intelligence and emotional mystique bring him the devotion of many men who are glad to surrender the last remnants of individuality. McGregor thus becomes the master of a terrifying collective force whose power can be exerted against society. The collective mass, rejecting the false premises of a democracy that is disorderly, will create a new order, a new mind. "When you have marched until you are one giant body then will happen a miracle," McGregor tells his followers. "A brain will grow in the giant you have made."

Had Anderson been able to stop the novel at that point, he would have written a meaningful indictment of American life and a warning of its self-destructiveness. Supporting the indictment are many valid social criticisms, some in the form of Anderson's authorial comments and others in passages of description and narration. His ideas on the shoddy ugliness of goods, homes, cities, and living patterns, on the inequitable character of law, on the avid quest for sensation, and on other problems of the day were pertinent for the early twentieth century and are still relevant in many respects. Anderson was echoing earlier protests by Melville, Thoreau, and Whitman; he was in tune with such perceptive contemporaries as Thorstein Veblen, Frank Lloyd Wright, and William James.

But though Anderson could objectively summon up the root causes for McGregor's Nietzschean nihilism, clearly portrayed as a negative philosophy, he paradoxically shared McGregor's faith in blind action. The novel struggles unsuccessfully to maintain equilibrium between Anderson's constructive critical temper and his unabashed impulse for collective physical violence and social destruction. As if to mark his inability to resolve the novel's chaotic lack of focus, Anderson dropped McGregor from his narrative before its close. The final chapter completes the book's disintegration. A foreshadowing of *Many Marriages* (1923), the conclusion whips up a mélange of sex and philosophy in portraying the success of a Chicago industrialist's effort to persuade his daughter that he is more desirable than McGregor, whom she has loved but to whom she has been afraid to give herself.

The idea and form of *Marching Men* were confused. But Anderson's style had progressed beyond the clumsy rawness of most of his earlier novel, had moved closer to the prose poetry of *Winesburg, Ohio*. His growing mastery of imaginative detail is visible in young McGregor's shocked perception that the coal-town minister is laughing callously at a cruel story about the boy: "The Reverend Minot Weeks also laughed. He thrust four fingers of each hand into the pockets of his trousers, letting the extended thumbs lie along the swelling waist line. From the front the thumbs looked like two tiny boats on the horizon of a troubled sea. They bobbed and jumped about on the rolling

shaking paunch, appearing and disappearing as laughter shook
him."

The urban scene evokes cold, sharp disgust: "The people of
Chicago go home from their work at evening — drifting they go
in droves, hurrying along. It is a startling thing to look closely
at them. The people have bad mouths. Their mouths are slack
and the jaws do not hang right. The mouths are like the shoes
they wear. The shoes have become run down at the corners
from too much pounding on the hard pavements and the mouths
have become crooked from too much weariness of soul. . . . It is
evening and the people of Chicago go home from work. Clatter,
clatter, clatter, go the heels on the hard pavements, jaws wag, the
wind blows and dirt drifts and sifts through the masses of the
people. Every one has dirty ears. The stench in the street cars
is horrible. The antiquated bridges over the rivers are packed
with people. The suburban trains going away south and west are
cheaply constructed and dangerous. A people calling itself great
and living in a city also called great go to their houses a mere
disorderly mass of humans cheaply equipped. Everything is cheap.
When the people get home to their houses they sit on
cheap chairs before cheap tables and eat cheap food. They have
given their lives for cheap things."

In opposition to that nightmare horror, Anderson chanted the
promise of nature in prophetic Biblical cadences: "And back
of Chicago lie the long corn fields that are not disorderly. There
is hope in the corn. Spring comes and the corn is green. It
shoots up out of the black land and stands up in orderly rows.
The corn grows and thinks of nothing but growth. Fruition
comes to the corn and it is cut down and disappears. Barns
are filled to bursting with the yellow fruit of the corn. And Chicago has forgotten the lesson of the corn. All men have

forgotten. It has never been told to the young men who come out of the corn fields to live in the city."

The invigorating effect of Gertrude Stein's experimentation with language in *Tender Buttons* is evident in *Marching Men.* Her theory is virtually summed up by Anderson in the novel: "It is a terrible thing to speculate on how man has been defeated by his ability to say words. The brown bear in the forest has no such power and the lack of it has enabled him to retain a kind of nobility of bearing sadly lacking in us. On and on through life we go, socialists, dreamers, makers of laws, sellers of goods and believers in suffrage for women and we continuously say words, worn-out words, crooked words, words without power or pregnancy in them."

For Anderson, Miss Stein always remained a "writer's writer," a literary pioneer, not a writer for the general reader. He recognized that her abandonment of conventional syntax, punctuation, and spelling was therapeutic for the American writer because it made him conscious of the deadness of conventional language and rhythm, of a literature based on literary custom rather than on objects, associations, functions, and speech freshly articulated. In 1914 such a revivification of style was needed. Gertrude Stein was a pioneer in the undertaking, soon to be joined by Anderson, Pound, Eliot, Joyce, the Dadaists, Cummings, Hemingway, and Faulkner. The poetic repetition and variation of words and phrases, the uncluttered images of objects, the varying musical beat and swing of sentences and paragraphs, noticeable in the passages quoted above from *Marching Men*, were stylistic techniques Anderson learned from her and passed along to Hemingway and Faulkner.

In the late fall of 1915, Anderson began to write the tales that make up *Winesburg, Ohio.* The majority were executed before the middle of 1916. A controlling plan apparently guided him, for the tales were composed in almost the sequence they occupy in the book. (An exception must be made for the four-part "Godliness," which Anderson salvaged from an unfinished novel of 1917.) The tales' unusual quality was recognized almost at once by "little magazine" editors in rebellion against the values dominating American letters and culture. Floyd Dell, Anderson's Chicago friend who helped arrange publication of *Windy McPherson's Son* and was an editor of *Masses*, printed three tales in 1916 beginning with "The Book of the Grotesque." Waldo Frank, editor with James Oppenheim and Van Wyck Brooks of *Seven Arts*, published four tales in 1916 and 1917. Two tales appeared in 1916 and 1918 respectively in the *Little Review*. Anderson had gained an audience that was small but appreciative of his lyrical prose.

William Phillips' study of the Winesburg manuscripts shows that Anderson wrote his first drafts with spontaneity and speed, and then polished with considerable care. The manuscript of "Hands," the second tale written, bears "almost two hundred instances in which earlier words and phrases are deleted, changed, or added to, to provide the readings of the final published version of the story." The revisions, ninety per cent of which were made after the initial writing, added to the size of the draft; they amplified the tale's subtlety by increasing its suggestive elements and symbolic content. The style was molded into greater informality by the addition of colloquial words and repetitive rhythms, and by the deletion of words that were "overworked or awkwardly used."

Much in the tales had prior existence in Clyde, Ohio, and Anderson's earlier life, thus justifying the subtitle: "A Group of Tales of Ohio Small Town Life." But the book, written in retrospect in Chicago, also reflects and illuminates urban American life. Winesburg as a microcosm is ultimately more than a national phenomenon; its proportions are universal, like the whale ship in Melville's *Moby Dick* and Faulkner's mythical Yoknapatawpha County.

The structure of *Winesburg, Ohio* was suggested by Edgar Lee Masters' *Spoon River Anthology*, an elegiac series of character sketches in poetry. The influence of Turgenev's *A Sportsman's Sketches*, in which a sympathetic but unsentimental narrator permits Russian character types to reveal themselves, is also evident. There are as well precedents for the book in nineteenth-century American literature, most notably the local-color collection of tales centered in a single geographical place, the obsessed monomaniacs of Hawthorne's fiction, and the mordant temper of E. W. Howe's *The Story of a Country Town*. The uniqueness of Anderson's book consists of the unusual quality of the precise, ironic voice offering delicate accounts of grotesque human creatures.

A partial key to the elegiac form and tone of the tales is embodied in the book's theory of the grotesque. At some distant time in the past, man had created and believed many satisfying, contradictory truths, "each truth . . . a composite of a great many vague thoughts." Then the healthy wholeness of a multiplicity of truths was lost; man picked out one particular truth, based his life upon it, and became a grotesque, his exclusive truth "a falsehood." The theory, like Hawthorne's statement in *The House of the Seven Gables* that in "an odd and incomprehensible world . . . a man's bewilderment is the measure of his wisdom," epitomizes the philosophy of uncertainty that dominated Anderson's thought and art: the "meaning of life" could not be defined by an absolute truth which limited man's possibilities, for the universe was open rather than closed. "Seeds," a tale first published in 1918, rounds out Anderson's theory by asserting that a confused woman who has mistaken selfish lust for selfless love "is a grotesque, but then all the people in the world are grotesques. We all need to be loved. What would cure her would cure the rest of us also. The disease she had is, you see, universal. We all want to be loved and the world has no plan for creating our lovers."

Everything in *Winesburg, Ohio* sets forth Anderson's vision of the grotesquerie of modern life, though in surrealistic rather than realistic fashion. The characters are deluded and solipsistic; they misunderstand themselves and others; they speak jerkily, explosively, mumblingly, or are inarticulate; their bodies are deformed or subject to muscular twitches, sometimes remain rigid while parts such as hands or feet move about independently. Frustrated, distorted, violent or passive, aggressive or self-destructive, the citizens of Winesburg are the living dead, victims of limited, life-denying truths and guilty for having chosen them.

The grotesques strive to tell their life stories to George Willard, young newspaper reporter. Their recitals are disjointed; their encounters with Willard episodic and inconclusive; his understanding of them incomplete. The tales are static episodes, empty of discovery and change. George Willard is on the whole a passive participant, himself a victim like the others, incapable of distinguishing between love and lust until the conclusion of the book, at which time he leaves Winesburg for a future that is dubious.

Anderson's subtle literary voice enriched the static nightmare of grotesquerie by infusing it with the dynamism of irony. The self-depreciating narrator struggles to be free of the limitations imposed upon him as a Winesburg grotesque. "And yet that is but crudely stated," he confesses humbly and typically in "Hands." "It needs the poet there." But it was as a truly great prose poet that Anderson took up the dormant literary tradition of mock oral narration, briefly revivified by Mark Twain, and transformed it afresh into a vibrant literary medium.

The book's narrator lacks the godlike knowledge and consequent arrogance of an omniscient author. Only to the extent that he artfully presents other grotesques, implying that he has attained an objective distance from them, will he transcend his grotesque configuration and justify his difficult effort to assume the role of artist rather than remaining a Winesburg zombie. The narrator, therefore, abjures sentimentality and pity as much as possible; his tenderness and sympathy are restrained and balanced with an astringent objectivity frequently brutal in contrast to the sufferings of his characters. The narrator's distance from his characters is established by reticence concerning physical details and by the use of a minimal amount of speech and scenic confrontation: the entangling possibilities of physical and dramatic immediacy are thus avoided. However, the narrator cannot help becoming subjectively involved. He observes, feels, digresses, analyzes, and generalizes. Yet he is often wrong, shortsighted, naive. He has become a major character in the tales who, like the symbolic objects liberally strewn about the pages of *Winesburg, Ohio*, must be metamorphosed into full meaning by the imaginatively stirred reader.

At the last, the narrator's stance of simple, artless sincerity revealing all is but a guise for artistic purpose and effect: all is actually given only as hint, clue, suggestion, implication, ambivalence, indirection. The covert truths proffered by Anderson never become didactic absolutes imposed by the narrator but remain implicit and open-ended. Each reader of the tales will grasp only as much of their essence as his individual insight is capable of apprehending.

Winesburg, Ohio is the first modern American expression of the wasteland theme later adumbrated in T. S. Eliot's *The*

Waste Land (1922), F. Scott Fitzgerald's *The Great Gatsby* (1925), Hemingway's *The Sun Also Rises* (1926), John Steinbeck's *To a God Unknown* (1933), and Nathanael West's *Miss Lonelyhearts* (1933), the latter, like Hemingway's novel, greatly indebted to Anderson's model. Unlike most of the writers who followed, Anderson attempted to fructify his wasteland, which symbolized the world of provinciality, gentility, and business he had rejected spiritually in his flight from Elyria to Chicago in 1913.

Winesburg, Ohio had delineated the arid context of Anderson's first life. Having given it aesthetic form, he believed it imperative to create — again in art — the context of his new life. The aim had been formulated with yearning simplicity by George Willard, like the new Anderson an artistic creation: "In every little thing there must be order, in the place where men work, in their clothes, in their thoughts. I myself must be orderly. I must learn that law. I must get myself into touch with something orderly and big that swings through the night like a star. In my little way I must begin to learn something, to give and swing and work with life, with the law."

The difficulties Anderson faced were great, particularly since he was still working on the Winesburg tales during 1916 and 1917, when he began his quest for new definitions, and the mood of Winesburg pervaded him. There was nothing in Winesburg as he had portrayed it, with the exception of nature, to which he could return; the ties which bound men in community had withered; love had degenerated into conflict, sexual repression, and disappointing lust; familial relations mirrored the larger social emptiness; the traditional reliances of religious orthodoxy and ritual modes of cultural behavior were nonexistent. He had cast aside the illusions of business and the ugliness of the city. In every respect, then, he was free and unattached, young in situation and possibility, ready to make the world live up to its fruitful potentialities and become a habitable place for human beings.

In actuality, of course, the matter was not so simple. Anderson was in his early forties, exuberant but also physically and mentally weary. As he later granted in his *Memoirs*, the Winesburg vision of his Ohio town had been harshly biased and he had too hastily rejected its few worthy attributes. It is apparent from the revelations in the early novels and the letters of this period that he had been psychically maimed by the experiences of his first forty years. Nor, regardless of how much will he exerted, could he easily slough off the worldliness of his mind, or easily assume the role of newborn infant or virginal adolescent after the mature triumph of his repudiation of business and familial ties, after the even greater triumph of having transformed himself into an accomplished artistic creator. The record of Anderson's Progress as a new Adam is inevitably a compilation of noble effort, heroic attainment, and pathetic failure. As it must have been for one who, as he wrote in the poetic epigraph of "From Chicago" (*Seven Arts,* May 1917), was a "man child, in America, in the west, in the great valley of the Mississippi . . . a confused child in a confused world."

Henceforth, Anderson's art and life were inseparable. Instead of remaining hidden behind his work like James Joyce, Anderson made the problem of self-understanding the focus of his best work. He found it as necessary to write about himself as an artist as to work at his art: "While he is still young and pregnant with life it behooves the artist who would stand unashamed among men to make his contribution to the attempt to extend the province of his art. And as his struggle as an artist is and must be inseparably bound up with his struggle as a man, the attempt may fairly be said to fall under the head of an effort to extend the possibilities of human life." So opens "From Chicago," but it concludes humbly on a foreboding note so strong that Anderson self-consciously omitted the section when reprinting the piece in *Sherwood Anderson's Notebook* (1926): "I am looking forward to the coming of the new artist who will give us . . . the beautiful and stirring story of the spirit that failed, just as the artist himself shall fail and who, like the Christ, on that dramatic night in the garden, must come at last to the facing of truth and know that he must always fail, that, even in keeping alive the memory of his struggle, all men shall fail." This tempering of egoism with limitation helped save Anderson from becoming, except briefly in the 1920's, a tiresome brayer of virtuous Self-hood in the manner of some of his less gifted imitators.

Mid-American Chants (1918), a collection of free-verse poems in the Whitmanian manner which Anderson began writing early in 1917, illustrates one phase of his attempt to fill his void. The poems are generally inept. Only a few manage coherently to unite their fragmentary rhapsodic ejaculations with the kind of sustained emotional energy, intellectual content, and symbolic structure present in Whitman's best poems. Anderson wanted to re-create the religious spirit and mythology of pagan Indian culture in the Ohio Valley before the culture's destruction by New England's pioneers. But he was insufficiently familiar with the details to do more than refer vaguely to the culture. On the other hand, when he did achieve a fragile identification, he blurred it with an alien prophetic exhortation and imagery derived from the Old Testament and Carl Sandburg. Not until Hart Crane wrote "The Dance" (*The Bridge*, 1930) were the primitive fertility rhythms of sacrifice, harvest, and rebirth celebrated in modern American poetry with the Dionysian richness Anderson sought to express.

Anderson was surprised that the editors of *Seven Arts* — one of whom, James Oppenheim, even wrote Whitmanesque poetry —

frowned upon the poems later collected in *Mid-American Chants*. The apocalyptic spirit of the magazine, which found hope for an American Renaissance in "self-expression without regard to current magazine standards" and eulogized Anderson in the first issue as an emergent Whitman, had diverted him from the disciplined temper governing the Winesburg stories. It had encouraged him to assume the role of ebullient national bard and to find in the seeds, roots, stalks, and husks of corn — the recurrent symbol of the chants — a means of ordering his chaos. However, the excesses which *Seven Arts* encouraged as one product of its doctrines were actually abhorrent to men like Frank and Brooks. Their most fervent aim was to awaken an idealistic national art rather than to discard traditional standards of literary taste and accomplishment. Anderson's friendship with these men and his respect for their judgment declined in the heat of argument, though he maintained his intimacy with them for some years thereafter.

"An Apology for Crudity" (*Dial*, November 8, 1917) was a manifesto of his independent literary position which sniped at the formalism of his *Seven Arts* critics and others who had ridiculed several poems that had appeared in *Poetry* (September 1917). Significant literature, he asserted, could only come after a writer's immersion in the life of his times. Since "crudity and ugliness" were prime characteristics of American industrial society, modern literature must be affected by it. He rejected, consequently, the "intellectuality" and "subtlety" of Henry James and William Dean Howells as ends in themselves, though he granted that both men were "American masters in prose." He linked himself to the tradition of Walt Whitman, Mark Twain, and Theodore Dreiser, who had not ignored the common.

But Anderson did not espouse realism. Vaguely he set forth the ideal of "subjective writing" as an alternative, the writer serving as an imaginative distiller of persons and experience. Later, in "A Note on Realism" (*New York Evening Post Literary Review*, October 25, 1924), he phrased his conception more concretely: "The life of the imagination will always remain separated from the life of reality. It feeds upon the life of reality, but it is not that life—cannot be. . . . Upon the fact in nature the imagination must constantly feed in order that the imaginative life remain significant. . . . The life of reality is confused, disorderly, almost always without apparent purpose, whereas in the artist's imaginative life there is purpose. There is determination to give the tale, the song, the painting Form—to make it true and real to the theme, not to life. Often the better the job is done the greater the confusion." Essentially, then, form and style were organic discoveries of imaginative creation, not pre-existent molds chosen in advance of the literary adventure.

Despite Anderson's impatience with the conventional novel and his recurrent effort to discover a "looser" form, his next major work failed to demonstrate any "experimental" characteristics. *Poor White* (1920) delineated the decline of the "pastoral golden age" in his Midwest during the 1880's and 1890's, the years of his childhood and adolescence. The book is crammed with information, for Anderson tried to anchor it in the facts of cultural, social, and economic history. Furthermore, he enveloped life in the Ohio town of Bidwell—which also appears in other post-Winesburg fiction—with a quiet charm derived from stable community relations, proximity to nature, intellectual curiosity and discussion, old houses, and streets shaded with old overhanging trees. Much of the vision is valid, but Anderson's nostalgia led him to idealize the town and its region until they became as exaggeratedly beautiful as Winesburg earlier had been exaggeratedly ugly. Yet this excessively rosy portrait of Bidwell was also aesthetically sound, for it enabled Anderson to dramatize the emotional and social significance of its degeneration into Winesburg.

The corrupting agent in the agrarian paradise was industrialism, which had elevated materialism and turned men into mechanical monsters. Hugh McVey, a Huckleberry Finn-type from the Mississippi River town of Mudcat Landing, Missouri, symbolically embodies the process. With unsparing realism, young McVey is shown to be a shiftless and lazy "poor white," redeemed, however, by his tendency to daydream and transcend himself pantheistically in sky, earth, and water.

Orphaned, McVey lives with a family which indoctrinates him with the virtues of industry and profit. Gradually he becomes wholly mathematical in mind and mechanical in spirit, channeling his imagination into the invention of labor-saving agricultural machinery. The machines bring him financial success even though, ironically, they turn out to be unworkable and thus symbolically fraudulent. They involve the town in a fever of speculation, disrupting all patterns of behavior, all relations. The novel contains many vivid episodes of the degenerative transformation of characters into tormented grotesques when they are suddenly deprived of the self-fulfilling creative tasks of old. In all of Bidwell, the only creatures who remain virile and sentient are horses. McVey is also a grotesque, unable to consummate his marriage because of psychic impotence, roused finally from his dehumanization by the beautiful appearance of some brightly colored stones he has found. At the end, after a symbolic attack upon McVey by a maddened handicraftsman, Hugh's patient wife — a "new woman" given to thinking rather than feeling — is roused to maternal womanliness by his reversion to adolescent helplessness. The novel grinds to a confusing halt as Hugh, stirred by "the disease of thinking," is told by "his woman" of the forthcoming arrival of "a man child." This news is greeted mockingly by "a great whistling and screaming" from Bidwell's factories.

The style of *Poor White* is effectively elegiac and muted as befits the portrait of an unrecoverable past. It is also generally free of the grammatical errors and poor punctuation that had marred *Winesburg, Ohio* slightly and to a greater extent the earlier novels. *Poor White* was the high point of Anderson's novelistic career. However, it represented a mere refinement of the structure and materials of *Windy McPherson's Son* and *Marching Men* rather than a significant advance. All three novels are essentially accounts of the distortion of a man in youth, his subsequent involvement in a maturity of social fraud and emotional impoverishment, his attempt to attain self-fulfillment in escape and love with an unsatisfactory woman who symbolizes reason and convention rather than emotion and revolt, and the uncertainty of the man's future at the conclusion.

Undoubtedly these novels served Anderson as self-analysis. But the requirements of their objective form kept him from venturing deeply into a personal probing that would have brought him profoundly into himself and encouraged analytical subtlety and particularized detail. The novels come perilously close to being true-confession literature in which the apparent openness of the writing hardly conceals the complacent obduracy with which the author reiterates rather than explores the troubles from which he supposedly has escaped.

Anderson's next novel, *Many Marriages* (1923), exemplifies the impasse to which such writing could lead; with its publication — it was initially printed serially in the *Dial* — came the first strong reaction against Anderson by the newer generation of American writers. Abandoning the chronological time sequence of the early novels, *Many Marriages* focused upon an extended moment of escape. This was given a past by means of flashbacks that vividly re-create the inhibition of feminine passion. But Anderson did little to set forth the positive hopeful quality of his masculine protagonist's passion beyond having him posture nakedly in presumably ritualistic fashion before a statue of the Virgin Mary. This ritual is neither primitive nor Catholic, for Anderson failed to provide any meaning for his key symbol, which he had picked up in *The Education of Henry Adams*. The result was a stasis, the temper of the Winesburg tales, that violated the thematic meaning of *Many Marriages* and revealed a disturbing lack of literary self-consciousness. What should have been a short story had been turned into a faulty novel.

Anderson published three more novels: *Dark Laughter* (1925), *Beyond Desire* (1932), and *Kit Brandon* (1936). All of them, like his preceding novels, have extraordinary scenes and passages whose high quality has been overlooked. These last novels also show that he endeavored to cope with the problems of extended narrative fiction in different ways; his solutions, however, were generally unsatisfactory, whether it was the attempt to portray the stream of consciousness in *Dark Laughter* or the device of having a central character relate her life story in an extended monologue in *Kit Brandon*.

Anderson's letters and writings from the mid-1910's until shortly before his death reveal that the objective novel, particularly the social novel, had interested him deeply only before the composition of the Winesburg tales. During the late 1910's, before the publication of *Poor White*, he began and abandoned several novels. After 1925, the pattern was repeated. His impulse was for expression in short forms: the poem, prose poem, and lyrical short story. But he was compelled, particularly since he had begun his career as a novelist, to continue writing novels. As late as 1933, for example, the publishing house of Scribner's invited him to become one of its authors with the stipulation,

33

according to Anderson, that the first of his books "must be either a novel or a continuous narrative."

It was not merely the pressure of publishers, as well as readers and critics, which pushed Anderson toward the novel against his natural inclination to work in shorter forms. Anderson shared the erroneous cultural belief that a novel is qualitatively as well as quantitatively more valuable than a short work. Had he been a younger man in the late 1910's and early 1920's, it is possible that he might have been able to develop the lyrical novel, a delicate form that would have best utilized his talents as it did those of Virginia Woolf, his admirer. But he had insufficient time in which to work slowly and perfect his art in every form. By 1919, at the age of forty-three, he was exhausted with the difficulty of earning his living as an advertising man and writing in his spare time. Not until 1922 did he finally leave the advertising business, convinced by the size of his earnings from books and magazines that he would be able to survive as a professional writer.

As it turned out, he was unprepared to work at the pace required of a professional writer whose contractual obligations force him to produce publishable materials on a regular basis. He wished to experiment, to work as the impulse to create arose, to make discoveries as any other young writer who still has his future ahead of him: Anderson believed that his life had begun in 1916 with the publication of his first book. Yet as a professional writer in the 1920's he allowed himself to publish whatever he wrote, regardless of whether or not he was proud of it. Thus he ironically was seduced by the same dream of success that he had repudiated in business.

Nevertheless, the bulk of Anderson's important creation is far greater than most critics and readers appear to have realized. His significant contribution to American literature begins with

Winesburg, Ohio and includes many pieces of prose and poetry published in books and magazines from 1916 to 1941. To that body of work should be added the successful chapters and sections from generally unsatisfactory books, as well as the luminous autobiographical sketches compiled in the posthumous *Memoirs*.

One reason Anderson's writing has not received full recognition, apart from the disappointment aroused by his novels, is the uneven character of his books. Anderson's eagerness to publish, encouraged by editors and publishers, is partially responsible. For example, the two books which crystallized his fame as a short fiction writer in the early 1920's —*The Triumph of the Egg* (1921) and *Horses and Men* (1923) — are mixtures of quality and dross. In both books he included pages salvaged from discarded novels which were on the whole below the level of his current work. "Unlighted Lamps" and "The Door of the Trap" (*The Triumph of the Egg*) are sections of novels begun before 1913. "A Chicago Hamlet" (*Horses and Men*) is a portion of a 1918 novel; "An Ohio Pagan" and " 'Unused' " in the same collection are parts of unpublished novels begun in 1920. A little more than half of *Horses and Men* thus belies the subtitle's description of the contents as "tales." Anderson's last collection of short fiction, *Death in the Woods* (1933), is similarly uneven. It should be noted, however, that the novel fragments frequently contain some of Anderson's most evocative writing. The pantheistic embrace of nature in "An Ohio Pagan," for example, has rarely been equaled in American literature.

Another reason for the relative neglect of Anderson's total accomplishment is the special nature of his talent. He wrote in an age which believed it could master the disorder of existence with patterns of order derived from myths and ideologies of the past or else with descriptions of objects and behavior that possessed the irreducible precision of scientific writing. Because

Anderson did not adopt either one of these solutions, his reputation was severely damaged during the 1920's. A reassessment is now in order, for his alleged weaknesses ironically have become strengths which link him with some of the most vigorous currents in contemporary literature. Anderson's vision and method reappear triumphantly in recent American literature in the writing of Carson McCullers, Bernard Malamud, Flannery O'Connor, Tennessee Williams, Edward Albee, Saul Bellow, and John Hawkes. Anderson's pioneering conglomeration of the picaresque, the antiheroic, the grotesque, the passionate, and the rebellious is no longer puzzling nor is it a sign of irresponsible "mindlessness."

One of the most interesting discoveries to be made is that sentimentality is not one of the chief characteristics of Anderson's writing. When dealing with characters whose suffering and confusion he delineated at excessive length, failing to complicate and particularize their uniqueness or to impart visible moral and intellectual significance to their predicaments, he did become pathetic and sentimental. Illustrations of his failure to claim the complex response of a reader are *Many Marriages* and "Out of Nowhere into Nothing."

But Anderson's critical temper conflicted strongly with his tendency toward acceptance and complacency. He could become exceptionally sharp, often brutal, in combating the impulse of quiescence. The lively battle he carried on elicited an amused, ironic attitude toward himself and his world. He often wrote satirically ("The Egg," 1920, and "The Triumph of a Modern, or, Send for the Lawyer," 1923) and often comically ("I'm a Fool," 1922, "There She Is — She Is Taking Her Bath," 1923, and "His Chest of Drawers," 1939). To have separated satire and comedy is misleading, however, for Anderson at his most humorous gives us that rare blend known as the tragicomic. When he achieved it, as in "The Egg," it rested in a delicate suspension of irony that looked back to the narrative voice of *Winesburg, Ohio.* Despite lapses into what Faulkner in 1925 described as an "elephantine kind of humor about himself," Anderson's vision remained deeply, incongruously tragicomic. Despite the dark years through which he passed in the late 1920's, this vision reemerged in his last decade of life, typically in his insistence in *Plays: Winesburg and Others* (1937) that the dramatized version of "The Triumph of the Egg" must be carefully directed in order to maintain a balance between comedy and tragedy; to play it either for "laughter" or "tears" alone would destroy the play.

Essentially Anderson was a lyric writer. Having accepted middle-class thought uncritically at first, then having rebelled against it, he feared that any other system of thought would be equally delusive, would limit and frustrate him, especially since reason tended to become abstract and to ignore the heart. "Feeling instinctively the uncertainty of life, the difficulty of arriving at truth," he resolved to remain "humble in the face of the great mystery" (" 'Unused,' " 1923). He might have been describing his own work when he wrote in *A Story Teller's Story*: "Dim pathways do sometimes open before the eyes of the man who has not killed the possibilities of beauty in himself by being too sure."

Anderson could be irritatingly blunt in stating his position, sneering at "slickness," "smartness," and glibness in all fields including literary criticism; thus he inevitably aroused charges of "mindlessness," "immaturity," and "distrust of ideas." Though he winced under the blows of increasingly harsh criticism, he unhesitatingly rejected ready-made truths of past and present. He turned his gaze inwards, searching for tentative explanations of mystery in the texture of his own emotional and social experience. His writings articulate the development of his perceptions of self in relation to the world, of the difficulties encountered on the way.

Anderson never abandoned the vision of himself as a poet despite the unfavorable reception of *Mid-Western Chants*, as late as 1930 writing an extraordinary prose poem in "Machine Song" (*Perhaps Women*, 1931). From 1919 to 1927 he assiduously wrote prose poems which appeared in magazines and *The Triumph of the Egg* and were collected in *A New Testament* (1927). He regarded this work at the outset as "a purely insane, experimental thing . . . an attempt to express, largely by indirection, the purely fanciful side of a man's life, the odds and ends of thought, the little pockets of thoughts and emotions that are so seldom touched." The poems on the whole are inchoate, too vague and incoherent to communicate more than faint hints of subconscious existence. But they were valuable exercises nonetheless. When Anderson turned to prose during this period, he passed beyond the mere undisciplined expression of self and made skillful use of poetic techniques which he never forgot.

As in *Winesburg, Ohio*, the varying perceptions of a poetically conceived narrator animate and unify most of Anderson's best stories, quite a few of which are products of the 1930's. For the sake of convenient reference, I cite only those stories that are easily accessible in one of Anderson's three collections and *The Sherwood Anderson Reader* (1947), though any comprehensive view of his work must also take into account many of his fine uncollected stories still available only in magazines: *The Triumph of the Egg*: "I Want to Know Why," "Seeds," "The Other Woman," "The Egg," and "Brothers"; *Horses and Men*: "I'm a Fool," "The Triumph of a Modern, or, Send for the Lawyer," "The Man Who Became a Woman," "Milk Bottles," "The Man's Story"; *Death in the Woods*: "Death in the Woods," "There She Is — She Is Taking Her Bath," "In a Strange

Town," "A Sentimental Journey"; *The Sherwood Anderson Reader*: "The Corn-Planting," "A Walk in the Moonlight," "The Yellow Gown," and "His Chest of Drawers." The first-person narrator sometimes merely introduces the monologue of another character, as in "The Other Woman" or "His Chest of Drawers." Only a few of Anderson's stories related from a third-person point of view possess high quality: "Senility" and "The New Englander" (*The Triumph of the Egg*), "Another Wife" and "Brother Death" (*Death in the Woods*), "Daughters" and "Not Sixteen" (*The Sherwood Anderson Reader*).

The uncertain, groping narrator of an Anderson story employs an art of suggestion to articulate his search for pattern and meaning in human existence. His experiences are fragmentary, incoherent, inexplicable. The chronological sequence of time may be interrupted and reversed by memories, inadvertent thoughts, gusts of emotion, and frustrated attempts at comprehension. Objects and people are haphazardly perceived, grotesquely distorted. Absurdly helpless, the narrator may succumb to impotence, give vent to explosive stirrings in his subconscious, flee the envelope of his body in mystical anguish or ecstasy, obsessedly focus upon trivialities such as a bent finger, find momentary relief in the muscular health and grace of animals.

Since the story is an articulation of the narrator's experience, its movement is repetitive and circular; it is not rounded off with a meaningful conclusion, for that would violate the narrator's integrity, his stance of wonder and search. Anderson's rejection of conventional plot and climax was aesthetically appropriate. So was his frequent representation of physical detail as incomplete image and generalized noun, his emphasis upon the musical sound of language before it becomes sense in order that he might portray the transformation of undifferentiated sensation and emotion into intelligible form.

The welter of sensuous and emotional perceptions is integrated — despite the powerful centrifugal impulse — by various unifying elements. The narrator maintains a consistent tone of voice. Whether youth or adult, light or serious, comic or satiric, critical or suppliant, he is also visibly interested and compassionate, anxious to discern the reality behind appearance. Moments in the story — episodes, sensations, repetitions — suddenly blaze up to give intense thematic illuminations. Objects, gestures, and events are encrusted with symbolic meaning. These symbols recur and invest the narrator's perceptions with deepened or new significance. Often these symbols are transformed into archetypal patterns of elemental human experience, such as sacrifice, initiation, and rebirth; Anderson's corn seed, for example, is a fertility symbol, its planting a ceremonial drama of death and resurrection.

Many of Anderson's stories, like his novels, are autobiographical either wholly ("In a Strange Town") or partially ("I Want to Know Why"). Presentation of a story from the first-person point of view encouraged an autobiographical concern. On the other hand, as a writer of autobiography, a form that fascinated him because of his vision of himself as "the American Man . . . a kind of composite essence of it all," he tended to fictionalize the details of his biography. This fusion of fact and fiction produced some of Anderson's finest lyrical prose. For example, "Death in the Woods," regarded as one of Anderson's best stories even by unfavorable critics, appeared as a third-person narrative (Chapter XII) in his autobiographical novel *Tar* (1926). In the same year, it also appeared as a story in the *American Mercury*; the name "Tar" had been replaced by "I" and third-person pronouns and other details revised to clarify the narrator's personal relations and experiences. "A Meeting South," the subtle account of Anderson's intimacy with Faulkner in New

Orleans, conceals Faulkner under a pseudonym and was probably read as fiction in the *Dial* (April 1925). It reappeared the next year as an autobiographical sketch in *Sherwood Anderson's Notebook* and finally was identified as a story in *Death in the Woods*. Anderson's autobiographical writings, which compose much of his total work, must be taken into account before any definitive conclusions about his literary significance can be ventured.

A starting point might well be Chapters X and XI of *Tar*, portrayals of horse racing as brilliantly colored and airy as Raoul Dufy's watercolors of French tracks, written in a supple vernacular that captures motion and youth with clear-eyed verve. Another excellent piece is "The Nationalist" (*Puzzled America*, 1935), a satirical dialogue with "the rat king of the South" who wants Congress to abolish the law protecting snowy egrets from shooting by feather-hunters. " 'It isn't the money I am thinking about,' he said. There was a grave injustice being done. 'These egrets,' he said again, 'are not American birds. They are foreign birds and they come up here only to eat our American fish.' " Two sketches, "White Spot" (1939) and "Morning Roll Call" (1940), both published posthumously in *The Sherwood Anderson Reader*, are brilliant examples of his ability to express himself during his last years with the vibrancy that had been a basis for his distinction during the early 1920's.

"White Spot" and "Morning Roll Call" had been intended for *Sherwood Anderson's Memoirs*, a work left unfinished when he died on March 8, 1941, in the Panama Canal Zone while on an unofficial goodwill tour to South America. According to James Schevill, the book was faultily edited by Paul Rosenfeld. Such sketches as "White Spot" and "Morning Roll Call" were omitted; a few random magazine pieces more than a decade old were included despite their incongruous misrepresentation of the style and aim of the autobiographical sketches Anderson wrote during the late 1930's and which constitute most of the volume. Unfinished though the book is, however, it represents a fitting culmination of his career. All of his earlier concern with self-revelation and stylistic nuance bore fruition in charming, lyrical pages that leave one in awe at the resiliency of the human spirit as it copes with the mysteries of being in art.

The vivacity and insight of Anderson's memoirs are remarkable in view of the severe decline of his reputation in the mid-1920's and the lengthy emotional depression that affected him thereafter. To those critics who did not read his works attentively or at all after 1925, when *Dark Laughter* appeared, and to those who know Anderson's writing only on the basis of *Winesburg, Ohio* and two over-anthologized stories — "I'm a Fool" and "I Want to Know Why" — the vibrancy of the memoirs will be truly inexplicable.

Perhaps Anderson should not have expected his work early or late to be wholly or widely appreciated. From the very beginning his literary reputation was shaky. Newspaper and magazine reviewers of his early books regularly oscillated between praise and blame, often mixing both.

Since Anderson was an avant-garde writer, however, a "little magazine" phenomenon, he was at first more enthusiastically received by young writers and critics interested in an American literature that was original, complex, unsentimental, and bold in dealing with taboo subjects such as sex. Thus young Hart Crane in 1921 wrote an encomium of Anderson's "paragraphs and pages from which arises a lyricism, deliberate and light, as a curl of milk-weed seeds drawn toward the sun. . . . He is without sentimentality; and he makes no pretense of offering solutions. He has humanity and simplicity that is quite baffling in depth and suggestiveness . . ."

42

But before long even the recognition of the avant-garde was qualified or withdrawn. It generally began to misjudge and overlook Anderson's method and to conclude mistakenly that he was an elderly, provincial American realist because he wrote about the Midwest and praised Dreiser for his human sympathy and his frankness in the treatment of sex. Anderson's persistent criticisms of Dreiser's style as clumsy and of Sinclair Lewis' style as superficial were ignored. The epitome of ultimate avant-garde response to Anderson is best seen in the pages of the *Dial*, which published him frequently, printed laudatory statements, and early in 1922 bestowed upon him the first *Dial* award for distinguished service to American letters, then in the next few years directly and allusively in reviews and other forms of comment gradually formulated a negative attitude toward him.

Anderson's rejection by the avant-garde deepened a sense of estrangement from vital currents of modern literature that had begun earlier when his first prominent supporters — Frank, Brooks, Paul Rosenfeld — kept finding fault with his theories and writings. In such works as *A Story Teller's Story* (1924), *The Modern Writer* (1925), and *Sherwood Anderson's Notebook* (1926), he hopefully sought to define and justify his credo. He was not helped in this task by his antipathy to "talk" about literature and ideas or by his aversion to systematic exposition. Much of what he said had the nub of good sense but it was insufficiently clarified, overcast with a playfulness inappropriate for the occasion, and gave the impression of being narcissistic self-praise of an aesthetic phenomenon superior to traditional morality and critical judgment. Self-consciously ironic and derisive references to the "modern" began to appear in his fiction and articles. An attempt to demonstrate superior "modernity" in *Dark Laughter* was a fiasco: its style, supposedly an emulation of that in James Joyce's *Ulysses*, revealed a misunderstanding of the stream-of-consciousness technique; its rendition of expatriate American experience in Europe was ludicrously uninformed and unperceptive.

The strongest blows against Anderson's prestige and well-being came from young writers whom he had befriended. Hemingway, in whom Anderson had discovered "extraordinary talent" in 1921 and whose *In Our Time* (1925) had been published as a result of Anderson's efforts, parodied Anderson in *The Torrents of Spring* (1926). Faulkner, whose *Soldiers' Pay* (1926) had also been published following Anderson's efforts, less publicly but just as sharply ridiculed Anderson in the foreword to *Sherwood Anderson & Other Famous Creoles* (1926), a book published in a limited edition in New Orleans.

For the rest of his life, from the mid-1920's on, Anderson engaged in a quest for rediscovery of the talent which seemed to have atrophied. F. Scott Fitzgerald had written: "To this day reviewers solemnly speak of him [Anderson] as an inarticulate, fumbling man, bursting with ideas — when, on the contrary, he is the possessor of a brilliant and almost inimitable prose style, and scarcely any ideas at all." Anderson perceived, with utter rightness, that there is no style without form, no form without content, that ideas are no more important than the evocative enunciation of experience. He had traveled much during his early years as an advertising man and now he resumed his travels. His second marriage had ended in divorce in 1924, two years after he left the advertising business; his third marriage broke down in 1929. Restlessly he went about the country, observing men and women, listening, attempting to regain the equilibrium of mind, emotion, and voice that had earlier produced his particular artistic vision. The idea that a permanent home might provide stability attracted him. In 1926 he built a house in the mountains of southwestern Virginia; for several years beginning in 1927 he edited two newspapers in the nearby town of Marion, Virginia. Meanwhile he continued to write stories and articles, to struggle desperately with new novels. He was often stricken with black, destructive moods, on one occasion even threw the manuscript of an unpublished novel out of a hotel window, but persisted in his search for orientation. In 1930 he fell in love with his future fourth wife; their marriage was successful. Slowly he regained his self-confidence, his talent, and his sense of humor. These are embodied in writings which swell the enduring corpus of his work beyond that already produced by 1926, writings in which he returned to the common people and locales he had earlier portrayed with similar irony, pity, and understanding.

The ultimate test of a writer's permanence is the power of his words to rekindle generations other than his own. Not until all of the fine writing which Anderson produced during the sixteen-year period after 1925 has been assembled and read will it be possible to undertake the "proper evaluation" for which Faulkner called. Meanwhile, an important place in American literary history seems assured. With characteristic humility Anderson himself had said in 1921 "that after all the only thing the present generation of men in America could expect to do is to make with their bodies and spirits a kind of fertilizing element in our soil." The issue of final grandeur and fame was a matter he left to others.

✒ Selected Bibliography

Works of Sherwood Anderson

NOVELS AND COLLECTIONS OF SHORT STORIES

Windy McPherson's Son. New York: John Lane, 1916. (Revised edition, New York: B. W. Huebsch, 1922.)

Marching Men. New York: John Lane, 1917.

Winesburg, Ohio: A Group of Tales of Ohio Small Town Life. New York: B. W. Huebsch, 1919.

Poor White. New York: B. W. Huebsch, 1920.

The Triumph of the Egg: A Book of Impressions from American Life in Tales and Poems. New York: B. W. Huebsch, 1921.

Horses and Men: Tales, Long and Short, from Our American Life. New York: B. W. Huebsch, 1923.

Many Marriages. New York: B. W. Huebsch, 1923.

Dark Laughter. New York: Boni and Liveright, 1925.

Beyond Desire. New York: Liveright, 1932.

Death in the Woods and Other Stories. New York: Liveright, 1933.

Kit Brandon: A Portrait. New York: Scribner's, 1936.

POETRY AND PLAYS

Mid-American Chants. New York: John Lane, 1918.

A New Testament. New York: Boni and Liveright, 1927.

Plays: Winesburg and Others. New York: Scribner's, 1937.

AUTOBIOGRAPHY AND OTHER PROSE

A Story Teller's Story: The Tale of an American Writer's Journey through His Own Imaginative World and through the World of Facts . . . New York: B. W. Huebsch, 1924.

The Modern Writer. San Francisco: Lantern Press, 1925.

Sherwood Anderson's Notebook. New York: Boni and Liveright, 1926.

Tar: A Midwest Childhood. New York: Boni and Liveright, 1926.

Hello Towns! New York: Liveright, 1929.

The American County Fair. New York: Random House, 1930.

Perhaps Women. New York: Liveright, 1931.

No Swank. Philadelphia: Centaur Press, 1934.

Puzzled America. New York: Scribner's, 1935.

A Writer's Conception of Realism. Olivet, Mich.: Olivet College, 1939.

Home Town. New York: Alliance, 1940.

Sherwood Anderson's Memoirs. New York: Harcourt, Brace, 1942.

The Sherwood Anderson Reader, edited with an Introduction by Paul Rosenfeld. Boston: Houghton Mifflin, 1947.

Letters of Sherwood Anderson, edited with an Introduction by Howard Mumford Jones in association with Walter B. Rideout. Boston: Little, Brown, 1953.

CURRENT AMERICAN REPRINTS

The Portable Sherwood Anderson, edited with an Introduction by Horace Gregory. New York: Viking Portable. $1.65.

Short Stories, edited with an Introduction by Maxwell Geismar. New York: American Century (Hill and Wang). $1.95.

Winesburg, Ohio, edited with an Introduction by Malcolm Cowley. New York: Compass (Viking). $1.45.

Bibliographies

Sheehy, Eugene P., and Kenneth A. Lohf. *Sherwood Anderson: A Bibliography*. Los Gatos, Calif.: Talisman Press, 1960.

Tanselle, G. Thomas. "Additional Reviews of Sherwood Anderson's Work," *Papers of the Bibliographical Society of America*, 56:358–65 (1962).

Critical and Biographical Studies

Adams, Richard P. "The Apprenticeship of William Faulkner," *Tulane Studies in English*, 12:113–56 (1962).

Anderson, David D. "Sherwood Anderson after 20 Years," *Midwest Quarterly*, 119–32 (1962).

Beach, Joseph Warren. *The Outlook for American Prose*. Chicago: University of Chicago Press, 1926.

Bishop, John Peale. "The Distrust of Ideas" [1921], in *The Collected Essays of John Peale Bishop*. New York: Scribner's, 1948.

Chase, Cleveland B. *Sherwood Anderson*. New York: McBride, 1927.

Crane, Hart. "Sherwood Anderson," *Double-Dealer*, 2:42–45 (1921).

Dahlberg, Edward. *Alms for Oblivion*. Minneapolis: University of Minnesota Press, 1964.

Duffey, Bernard. *The Chicago Renaissance in American Letters*. Lansing: Michigan State College Press, 1954.

Faulkner, William: "Sherwood Anderson: An Appreciation," *Atlantic Monthly*, 191:27–29 (1953).

Fenton, Charles A. *The Apprenticeship of Ernest Hemingway*. New York: Farrar, Straus, 1954.

Fitzgerald, F. Scott. "How to Waste Material: A Note on My Generation," *Bookman*, 63:262–65 (1926).

Frank, Waldo. "Emerging Greatness," *Seven Arts*, 1:73–78 (1916).

Gregory, Alyse. "Sherwood Anderson," *Dial*, 75:243–46 (1923).

Herbst, Josephine. "Ubiquitous Critics and the Author," *Newberry Library Bulletin*, 5:1–13 (1958).

"Homage to Sherwood Anderson," *Story*, Vol. 19 (September–October 1941). (Contributions by James Boyd, Van Wyck Brooks, Theodore Dreiser, Waldo Frank, Julius W. Friend, Lewis Galantière, Harry Hansen, Henry Miller, Paul Rosenfeld, William Saroyan, Gertrude Stein, Thomas Wolfe, and others.)

Howe, Irving. *Sherwood Anderson*. New York: Sloane, 1951.

Phillips, William L. "How Sherwood Anderson Wrote *Winesburg, Ohio*," *American Literature*, 23:7–30 (1951).

Rosenfeld, Paul. "Sherwood Anderson," *Dial*, 72:29–42 (1922).

Schevill, James. *Sherwood Anderson: His Life and Work*. Denver: University of Denver Press, 1951.

"Sherwood Anderson Number," *Shenandoah*, Vol. 13 (Spring 1962). (Articles by James K. Feibleman, Frederick J. Hoffman, Jon S. Lawry, Walter B. Rideout, and Cratis D. Williams.)

"Sherwood Anderson Memorial Number," *Newberry Library Bulletin*, Second Series, No. 2 (December 1948). (Articles by George H. Daugherty, Waldo Frank, Norman Holmes Pearson, and Roger Sergel.)

Sutton, William A. Four articles on Anderson's life from 1884 to 1896 and 1899 to 1907, in *Northwest Ohio Quarterly*, 19:99–114 (1947), 20:20–36 (1948), 22:39–44 (1950), 22:120–57 (1950).

Trilling, Lionel. *The Liberal Imagination*. New York: Viking, 1950.

Walcutt, Charles C. *American Literary Naturalism, A Divided Stream*. Minneapolis: University of Minnesota Press, 1956.

Warren, Robert Penn. "Hawthorne, Anderson and Frost," *New Republic*, 54:399–401 (1928).

Weber, Brom. "Anderson and 'The Essence of Things,'" *Sewanee Review*, 59:678–92 (1951).

Wright, Austin McGiffert. *The American Short Story in the Twenties*. Chicago: University of Chicago Press, 1961.